W9-BCM-597

A my name is ALICE

by JANE BAYER * pictures by STEVEN KELLOGG

Dial Books for Young Readers

E. P. Dutton, Inc.   New York

Published by Dial Books for Young Readers
A Division of E. P. Dutton, Inc.
2 Park Avenue
New York, New York 10016

Library of Congress Cataloging in Publication Data
Bayer, Jane. A my name is Alice.
Summary: The well-known ball bouncing ditty that is
built on letters of the alphabet is illustrated
with animals from all over the world.
1. Jump rope rhymes. [1. Jump rope rhymes.
2. Alphabet. 3. Animals—Fiction.]
I. Kellogg, Steven, ill. II. Title.
PZ8.3.B342My 1984   398'.8   84-7059
ISBN 0-8037-0123-3
ISBN 0-8037-0124-1 (lib. bdg.)

Printed in the U.S.A.
First Edition
COBE
10 9 8 7 6 5 4 3 2 1

The full-color paintings are prepared using ink and
pencil line with watercolor washes.
Then they are camera-separated and reproduced
in red, yellow, blue, and black halftones.

For Carl, Zach, and Emmy
J.B.

For Jessica Easton Edwards with love
S.K.

my name is Alice and my husband's name is Alex.
We come from Alaska and we sell ants.

Alice is an APE.   Alex is an ANTEATER.

B

my name is Barbara and my husband's name is Bob.

We come from Brazil and we sell balloons.

Barbara is a BEAR.   Bob is a BABOON.

 **C** my name is Clara and my husband's name is Claude.

We come from Calcutta and we sell cakes.

Clara is a COW.   Claude is a CONDOR.

 **D** my name is Doris and my husband's name is Dave.

We come from Denmark and we sell dust.

Doris is a DUCK.   Dave is a DACHSHUND.

my name is Emily and my husband's name is Edward.

We come from Egypt and we sell eggs.

Emily is an EMU.   Edward is an ECHIDNA.

my name is Fifi and my husband's name is Fred.

We come from France and we sell feathers.

Fifi is a FOX.   Fred is a FROG.

**G** my name is Gertrude and my husband's name is George.

We come from Glasgow and we sell giggles.

Gertrude is a GOOSE.   George is a GORILLA.

my name is Hannah and my husband's name is Henry.

We come from Hawaii and we sell harps.

Hannah is a HIPPOPOTAMUS.   Henry is a HAMSTER.

I

my name is Ida and my husband's name is Ivan.

We come from Iceland and we sell ice cream.

Ida is an IBIS.   Ivan is an IBEX.

J my name is Jane and my husband's name is John.

We come from Japan and we sell jumpsuits.

Jane is a JACKAL.   John is a JACKRABBIT.

K my name is Karen and my husband's name is Keith.

We come from Kashmir and we sell kisses.

Karen is a KANGAROO.

Keith is a KIWI.

L

my name is Lucy and my husband's name is Luke.

We come from London and we sell leaves.

Lucy is a LEMMING.   Luke is a LOON.

my name is Maude and my husband's name is Martin.
We come from Manchester and we sell mops.

Maude is a MOOSE.   Martin is a MOLE.

N my name is Nancy and my husband's name is Ned.

We come from New York and we sell noodles.

Nancy is a NUTRIA.

Ned is a NEWT.

 my name is Olivia and my husband's name is Oscar.

We come from Ohio and we sell oatmeal.

Olivia is an OTTER.   Oscar is an OWL.

P

my name is Polly and my husband's name is Paul.

We come from Pittsburgh and we sell pebbles.

Polly is a PUFFIN.   Paul is a PIG.

my name is Queenie and my husband's name is Quentin.

We come from Quebec and we sell question marks.

Queenie is a QUAIL.

Quentin is a QUAHOG.

**R** my name is Rosie and my husband's name is Richard.

We come from Rome and we sell rubbish.

Rosie is a RHINOCEROS.   Richard is a RAT.

 my name is Sally and my husband's name is Steve.

We come from Spain and we sell suntans.

Sally is a SERVAL.   Steve is a STORK.

T my name is Theresa and my husband's name is Ted.

We come from Thailand and we sell teeth.

Theresa is a TURKEY.   Ted is a TIGER.

 my name is Ursula and my husband's name is Ulysses.

We come from Uganda and we sell umbrellas.

Ursula and Ulysses are both UNAUS.

**V** my name is Virginia and my husband's name is Vinnie.

We come from Vermont and we sell vegetables.

Virginia is a VOLE.   Vinnie is a VULTURE.

 my name is Winifred and my husband's name is William.

We come from Wales and we sell whistles.

Winifred is a WOLF.

William is a WEASEL.

 my name is Xena and my husband's name is Xavier.

We come from Planet Xigert and we sell Xofersizers.

Xena and Xavier are both XIGERTLINGS.

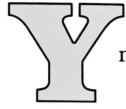 my name is Yolanda and my husband's name is Yancie.

We come from Yugoslavia and we sell yellow.

Yolanda and Yancie are both YAKS.

**Z** my name is Zelda and my husband's name is Zach.

We come from Zambia and we sell zippers.

Zelda is a ZEBRA.   Zach is a ZEBU.

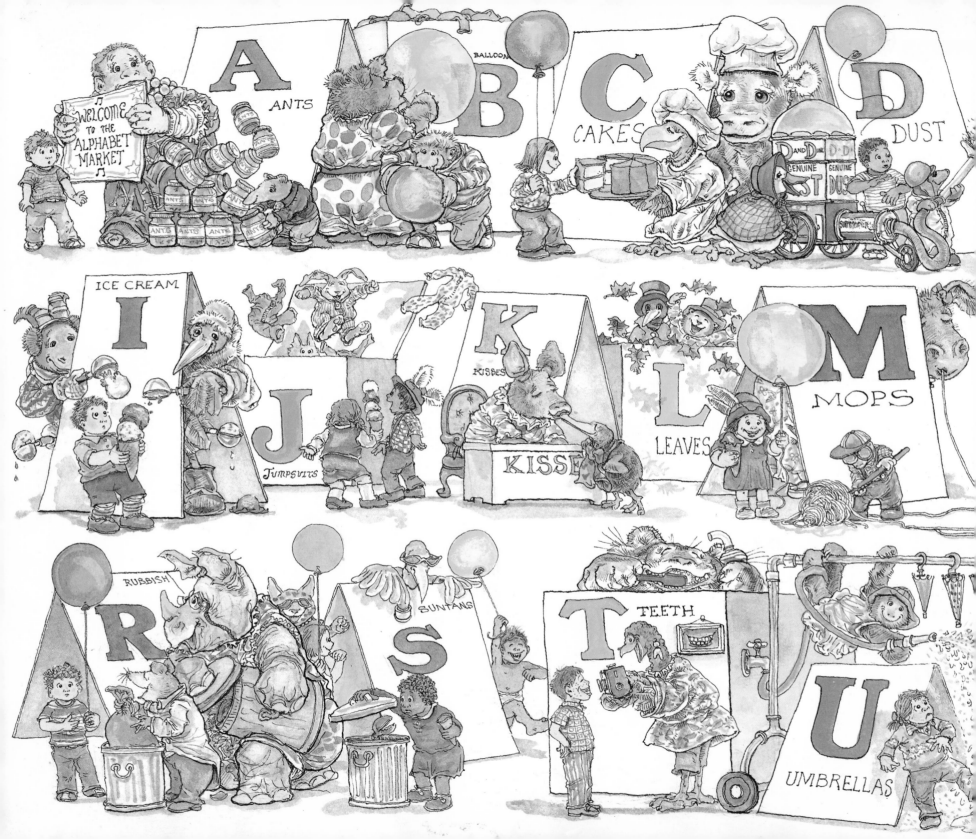

Some facts about less familiar creatures in A, my name is ALICE

CONDOR · a very large American vulture

EMU · a tall flightless bird

ECHIDNA · a burrowing rodent of Australia, Tasmania, and New Guinea

IBIS · a wading bird related to the herons

IBEX · a wild goat living in high mountain areas of the Eastern Hemisphere

KIWI · a flightless New Zealand bird

LEMMING · a small furry-footed rodent

LOON · a large fish-eating diving bird

NEWT · a small semiaquatic salamander

NUTRIA · a South American aquatic rodent

PUFFIN · a diving seabird having a short bill

QUAHOG · a thick-shelled American clam

QUAIL · a small game bird related to the partridge and pheasant

SERVAL · a long-legged African wildcat

UNAU · a two-toed tree-inhabiting mammal

VOLE · a small rodent related to muskrats and lemmings

YAK · a large long-haired ox

XIGERTLING · a good-natured long-necked creature native to the planet Xigert and part of a universe that has not yet been born

ZEBU · an Asian ox

Author's Note

The alphabet text for this book comes from a playground game I learned in grammar school in the early fifties. The game was played by bouncing a ball, one bounce for each word. And each time a word beginning with the correct letter of the alphabet came up, the player had to put one leg over the ball as it bounced. The object was to think of names and places and things to sell for each letter of the alphabet and *not* to miss the ball.

The uniqueness of playground games—whether they are clapping games, jump rope rhymes, or ball bouncing games—is that they are taught by one child to another without the more formal instruction that an adult, such as a parent or teacher, would provide. The reason for this is not completely clear since adults in general pass on many children's songs and rhymes; but perhaps it is as simple as the fact that adults just don't like to play children's games. In any case it is clear that many of these playground ditties remain eternal—thirty years after I learned them, my children bring them home to me. Generation after generation, they never seem to leave the world of the child.

Jane Bayer